CONTENTS

 LOOK FOR THE FLYER

Look for the flying creature logo in boxes like this.
Here you will find extra facts and other
items of interesting information.

DAWN OF FLIGHT

Insects were the first flyers on Earth. They developed wings more than 300 million years ago, long before any other flying creature appeared.

▲ Apart from their smaller size, today's dragonflies look much like this ancient fossilised insect.

Three hundred million years ago, the steamy air over vast lush forests was filled with flying insects. One of the biggest prehistoric flyers was the *Meganeura*. This huge dragonfly had a wingspan of 70 cm.

    Meganeura was probably the deadliest flying hunter of the time. Its big eyes spotted prey easily, and its huge wings gave it enough speed for a quick chase. *Meganeura* used its six strong legs to catch an insect in midair. It ate its prey in flight while looking for another victim!

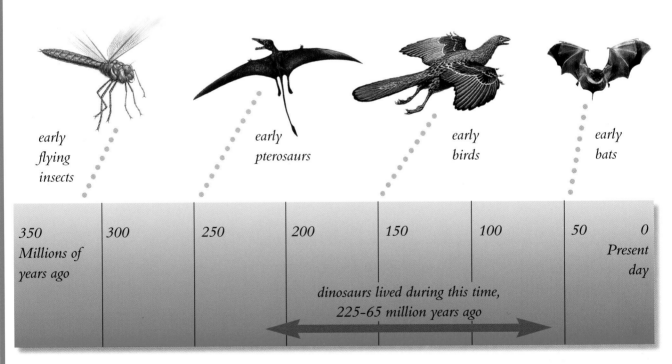

early flying insects   early pterosaurs   early birds   early bats

350 Millions of years ago	300	250	200	150	100	50	0 Present day

dinosaurs lived during this time, 225-65 million years ago

▲ Insects were the first animals to fly, followed by pterosaurs, birds and bats.

PREHISTORIC ANIMALS

FLYING CREATURES

MICHAEL JAY

Chrysalis Children's Books

First published in the UK in 2003 by
(b) Chrysalis Children's Books
an imprint of Chrysalis Books Group Plc
The Chrysalis Building, Bramley Rd,
London W10 6SP

ISBN 1 84138 890 4

British Library Cataloguing in Publication Data
for this book is available from the British Library.

Printed in China
10 9 8 7 6 5 4 3 2 1

Acknowledgements
We wish to thank the following individuals
and organisations for their help and assistance
and for supplying material in their collections:
Alpha Archive: 4 (tl), 5 (bl), 7 (br), 8, 15 (tr),
18 (bl), 21 (t), 24 (b), 27 (br), 30
Bernard Thornton Artists/Colin Newman:
4 (bl), 5 (t), 22 (b), 25 (tr)
Gavin Page: 3
John Sibbick: all other illustrations

Editorial Manager: Joyce Bentley
Design and editorial production:
Alpha Communications
Educational advisor: Julie Stapleton
Text editor: Veronica Ross

▲ In this scene from
170 million years ago,
a *Rhamphorynchus*
flying reptile snatches
a fish from a lake. An
adult *Rhamphorynchus*
had a wingspan of
about 1.5m.

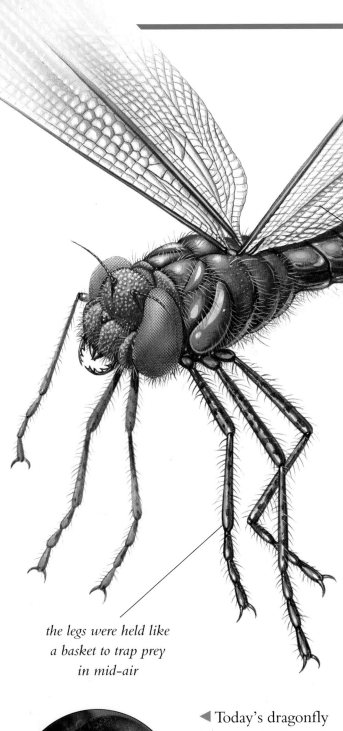

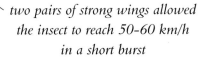

*two pairs of strong wings allowed
the insect to reach 50-60 km/h
in a short burst*

◄ *Meganeura* was probably the biggest insect that has ever flown. A dragonfly today has a wingspan of only 10 cm or so.

*the legs were held like
a basket to trap prey
in mid-air*

◄ Today's dragonfly has eyes similar to its ancestor's. They are called compound eyes and are made up of hundreds of tiny lenses, instead of a single big one.

HARD EVIDENCE

Researchers find out about animals of the distant past by looking at fossils, the hardened remains of dead creatures preserved in rock over millions of years.

However, only a few animals ever turn into fossils. Most of them were eaten by other animals or decomposed in the open air after dying. Often, just a few bones are found rather than a complete skeleton, or the remains may be a 'trace' fossil – for example, a set of footprints. Delicate insects may leave only an impression in the rock.

Even so, experts can often work out what an animal looked like and how it had lived.

REPTILE GLIDERS

Gliding reptiles existed 250 million years ago. They had extra-long ribs that stuck out on both sides of their bodies, supporting 'wings' made of skin.

lightweight skull

ribs

▲ *Coelurosauravus* glided through the sky. It probably snatched insects to eat in midair.

The *Coelurosauravus* was a 40 cm-long reptile that lived in prehistoric forests. Only a few remains of *Coelurosauravus* have been found, but they show that its 21 ribs could unfold, like a fan. When the ribs were spread open, a wing was formed that allowed the *Coelurosauravus* to make long, gliding flights from the treetops.

There are gliding reptiles alive today that look like *Coelurosauravus*. The *Draco volans* is a lizard from southeast Asia. It has only a few ribs, but they also unfold to make a wing for gliding flights of 50m or more.

The 10cm-long *Longisquama* was another prehistoric gliding reptile. It had a set of very long bony plates on its back that folded up like butterfly wings.

To glide through the air, the *Longisquama* leapt off a high branch and snapped open its backbone plates to make an instant wing.

▲ *Longisquama probably flicked its tail from side to side in midair to help it steer.*

Draco volans *is a present-day reptile that has changed little in millions of years*

 WHAT IS A REPTILE?

Reptiles are among the oldest animal groups. They usually have a covering of scales or horny plates, rather than fur or hair. Unlike mammals, they lay shelled eggs on dry land instead of giving birth to live young. Reptiles are also cold-blooded. They need heat from the Sun to be active. Mammals, such as humans, are warm-blooded. We can keep warm and active even in bitterly cold weather.

THE FIRST PTEROSAURS

Pterosaurs were strange flying reptiles that were masters of the air millions of years ago. There were many kinds of pterosaur – some were huge, others could fit in your hand.

◀ There are many well-preserved fossils of pterosaurs. This one was found in China in 2002.

Peteinosaurus *probably snatched insects in midair*

Long before birds, pterosaurs were the biggest flying creatures on Earth. Remains of the oldest known pterosaur were found in northern Italy in 1971. This pterosaur, named *Eudimorphodon*, is thought to have lived around 220 million years ago, at about the same time as early dinosaurs.

Eudimorphodon was a long-tailed animal, with a wingspan of about 1m. Its jaw was only as long as your forefinger, yet there were 114 teeth lining its narrow beak.

EATING IN THE AIR

Many pterosaurs flew well enough to catch flying insects in midair and *Eudimorphodon* could also catch fish easily. Flying low above the water, its sharp eyes could spot small fish swimming near the surface. Then, all *Eudimorphodon* needed to do was dip its beak into the water as it swooped overhead and snap up the fish with its needle-sharp teeth.

prehistoric dragonflies made a tasty catch

▼ Pterosaurs hunt for food 220 million years ago. The ones shown here ate mainly insects or fish.

Eudimorphodon *had sharp teeth that helped it catch small fish*

HAIRY FLYERS

Pterosaurs were reptiles, but unlike any reptile today, their bodies were not covered with scales. Instead, they had body hair, which was warm and light in weight.

furry body hair

Sordes had only a few teeth, but they were as sharp as needles

▲ *Sordes* may have rested in trees and shrubs. It folded its wings just like a modern bat.

In the 1960s, a Russian researcher found pterosaur remains that were far better preserved than any found before. They were detailed enough to show that this pterosaur had a furry coat of fine hair, up to 6 mm long.

The 63 cm-wingspan flyer was named *Sordes pilosus*, Latin words that mean 'hairy evil spirit'.

sharp eyesight helped Sordes hunt for insects

▲ *Sordes* had wings that looked rather like those of a bat. The wings were made of very thin skin.

Experts now agree that even though pterosaurs were reptiles, most kinds had some hair on their bodies. A scaly reptile, such as a snake, needs heat from its surroundings to be warm and active. A pterosaur's body hair may have been warm enough to keep it active, even in cool weather.

Sordes had features like many other pterosaurs – arms and legs supported its wings, a long tail helped steering.

 TREASURE TROVE

One of the best places for fossils is in the Karatau mountains of Kazakhstan, a country that borders the Caspian sea in Asia. Here researchers have found fossils of ancient insects that show every detail of their gauzy wings. The area is good for finding pterosaurs too, and this is where *Sordes* was discovered. Its remains were so perfectly preserved that every hair could be seen, even the short, downy ones between its toes!

NESTING PLACES

Did pterosaurs look after their young like birds do? Experts don't really know for sure, but they have some ideas of a pterosaur's home life.

◀ *Quetzalcoatlus* may have pecked at the bodies of dead animals, taking away tasty bits of food to feed its hungry young.

Dimorphodon *had a beak that is similar to that of a modern puffin*

Pterosaurs may have mated like birds, pairing off for a season – or even for life – and laying their eggs in a safe spot.

After they hatched, baby pterosaurs were as small and helpless as bird chicks, so the parents probably took care of them until they learnt to fly.

▶ *Dimorphodon* lived about 205 million years ago. Here a pair are shown spreading their wings in the Sun, basking on their 'nest rock'.

FEEDING TIME

Pterosaurs probably worked hard to feed their young. A fish-eater, such as the *Ornithocheirus*, may have brought back newly caught prey to its young, feeding them directly from the pouch in its throat.

parent pterosaur

We do not know if pterosaurs built nests like birds. They would have had homes though, such as a comfortable flat rock or a ledge on a cliff face. Some pterosaurs might have lived in colonies, like many sea birds today.

stiff tail with rudder at the end

arms were strong enough for rock climbing

STRANGE EATERS

The jaws of pterosaurs came in many shapes and sizes, depending largely on how the various kinds of pterosaur hunted for food.

▲ The pointed jaws of the *Dsungariterus* may have probed for small water creatures hiding in cracks under rocks.

Most pterosaurs ate fish or insects and had lots of sharp teeth to grab their prey on the move. But some pterosaurs were different. The *Pterodaustro* fed while standing up, sieving water for food with its weird beak.

head moved from side to side when sieving water for food

▶ Remains of *Pterodaustro* have been found in South America, where it lived 140 million years ago. An adult's wings stretched about 1.3m.

MODERN FILTER FEEDER

The water-sieve jaws of the *Pterodaustro* may seem odd, but other animals have also used this way of eating. A modern example is the flamingo, which feeds with its head upside down. The flamingo dips its beak in the water, then swings its head from side to side. Its tongue squeezes the water out of its beak, trapping food in fine sieves called platelets. Some flamingos eat mostly plants, others enjoy shrimps. Both these foods contain pink colouring which enters the flamingo's body, turning its feathers pale pink!

when the jaws were closed, the bristles stuck up, like a toothbrush

The *Pterodaustro*'s lower jaw had no teeth. Instead, it contained nearly 1000 bristles. These allowed the creature to filter food, such as tiny shrimps or water plants, from the water in its beak. The food was crunched up by small teeth in the *Pterodaustro*'s upper jaw before being swallowed.

CRESTED KILLERS

Large pterosaurs had long wings that let them glide easily in rising air currents. Some also had strange head crests to help them balance in flight.

▲ *Pteranodon ingens* soared on wings 7m across, yet it was very lightly built, weighing just 17 kg.

The biggest pterosaurs probably lived like today's soaring seabirds, such as the albatross. This bird spends most of its time gliding on air currents far from land. Pterosaurs could also glide long distances, an occasional flap of their huge wings being enough to keep them airborne.

Zooming over the sea at up to 50 km/h, a pterosaur could snatch a fish out of the water and gulp it down in a flash. A bony head crest may have helped to balance the weight of a long beak. It's likely, too, that at mating time, pterosaurs would have shown off their crests when competing for partners.

CREST VARIETY

Here are just four of the many pterosaur crests that have been found so far:

Anhanguerra

Gnathosaurus

Tropeognathus

Ctenochasma

16

pterosaur jumps off the cliff into rising air currents in order to fly

pterosaur dives to pick up speed before levelling out to hunt prey

Pteranadon sternbergi had a club-shaped crest

▲ Groups of pterosaurs may have nested in cliffside colonies.

GIANT OF THE SKIES

Quetzalcoatlus **was one of the biggest flying creatures that has ever existed. Its huge wings stretched up to 12m across!**

The huge *Quetzalcoatlus* was one of the last kinds of pterosaur. It lived far from the sea, spending its time circling over inland hills and valleys.

    Experts are not sure what this giant pterosaur ate. It may have lived like a vulture, pecking at dead carcasses, or perhaps it used its long beak to probe for food in pools and streams. For all its size though, *Quetzalcoatlus* was very lightly built. An adult weighed only about 86 kg, similar to a human adult.

▼ *Quetzalcoatlus* soars high over a herd of dinosaurs.

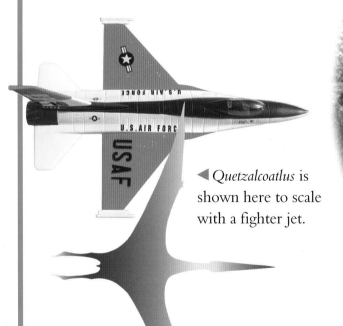

◄ *Quetzalcoatlus* is shown here to scale with a fighter jet.

thin wing has a
downy covering

WHAT HAPPENED TO THE PTEROSAURS?

All pterosaurs, including Quetzalcoatlus, died out about 65 million years ago, at the same time as the dinosaurs. Most experts think there were several reasons for this. For many years, huge volcanoes polluted the air with poisonous gas. Then a giant meteor crashed into the Earth, sending out huge tidal waves of boiling water. The heat wave and resulting climate changes killed off the pterosaurs, as well as many other plants and animals.

lightweight bones
formed the wing's
front edge

feet trailed straight out
behind, with no long tail

THE FIRST BIRD

Remains of the earliest-known bird were found in Germany in 1861. They showed a creature the size of a pigeon, with feathered wings and tail.

▲ *Archaeopteryx* lived at the same time as the fierce *Allosaurus* dinosaur.

▼ *Archaeopteryx* had the build of a dinosaur, but the front limbs of a bird.

The animal was named *Archaeopteryx* ('ancient wing'). It lived nearly 150 million years ago, at the same time as many pterosaurs and dinosaurs, and looked similar to a modern bird.

front claw

DINOBIRDS OF CHINA

Fossils discovered in northeast China since 1996 have shown that modern birds are descended from meat-eating dinosaurs.

The Chinese fossils are older than the *Archaeopteryx* and form a missing link that helps scientists work out how *Archaeopteryx* and today's birds developed from dinosaurs.

The most well-known Chinese fossil was found in 2000. It was named 'Fuzzy raptor' for its feathery coat, preserved clearly in the stone. It probably used its wing-like arms to grab at prey as it ran along the ground.

▲ The 'fuzzy raptor' fossil shows its front claws. These could snap forwards in a movement similar to that used by a bird at the start of a wing stroke.

We are not sure if *Archaeopteryx* flew as easily as a bird of today. Some experts think its wings were too small for long flights, so it is possible that *Archaeopteryx* spent most of its time on the ground. It could have run after prey (such as a small lizard) using its wings to scoop up the cornered animal.

Archaeopteryx may also have climbed trees, using its sharp claws to grip the trunk. From high in the branches, it could swoop down in a silent attack to grab its prey.

MEGABIRDS

adult Gastornis
and human to scale

Some prehistoric birds had such tiny wings they could not fly at all. But, many of these flightless birds were deadly giants that hunted other animals.

▲ Even an adult human would have been outsized by a grown *Gastornis*. The huge bird was taller, heavier and faster than any human.

The huge *Gastornis* was a fierce, flightless bird that lived more than 40 million years ago, after the pterosaurs and dinosaurs had died out. It stood over 2m tall, weighed almost half a tonne and had a large, hooked beak that could slash through flesh and crush bones to dust.

Gastornis was probably the deadliest killer of its time, and there was little other animals could do to defend themselves, except run or climb up a tree. *Gastornis* may have hunted prey such as the *Propalaeotherium*, an early ancestor of today's horse. But this animal was far smaller than a horse – it grew no bigger than a modern dog!

GIANT-SIZED FISHERBIRD

Baptornis was a 2m-long diving bird that lived millions of years before *Gastornis*, at the same time as many pterosaurs.

Baptornis could not use its tiny wings to fly – they were far too small for this. Instead, they were used as fins to help *Baptornis* steer under water. The bird's extra large, webbed feet gave it a high turn of speed when chasing fish.

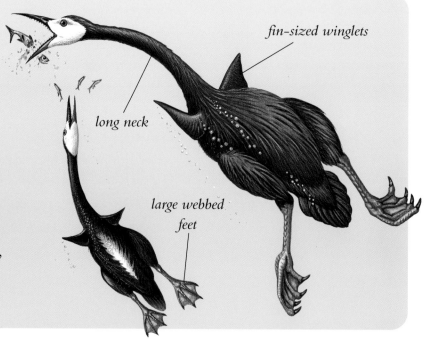

fin-sized winglets

long neck

large webbed feet

this early horse was tiny compared with a horse of today

Remains of *Gastornis* have been found in various places, including Germany and the USA. It was not the only giant flightless bird though – later kinds included the *Phorusrhacos* of South America, which was even bigger. This hunting bird grew up to a towering 3m high!

▲ *Gastornis* lived when Earth was warmer than now. Much of our planet was covered in jungle.

23

WINGS ACROSS THE WORLD

Birds were not alone in the air after the pterosaurs died out. In addition to many kinds of flying insect, there were early bats with tails and claws.

Bats were the fourth kind of animal to have wings that could flap, after insects, pterosaurs and birds. The oldest bat remains found are about 50 million years old. We think that the first bats developed from tree-dwelling mammals that glided between branches to grab insects in midair.

The early bat *Icaronycteris* looked quite similar to bats today, but there were some differences, including a long tail, a 'thumb' claw on each wing and more teeth.

bat

bird

pterosaur

▲ The wings of three flying creatures show how each is supported by an extended 'arm' and 'hand'.

▶ Like today's bats, *Icaronycteris* sent out high-pitched squeaks to find prey in the dark. Super-sensitive ears can hear echoes reflected back from objects around, so the bat can tell exactly where they are.

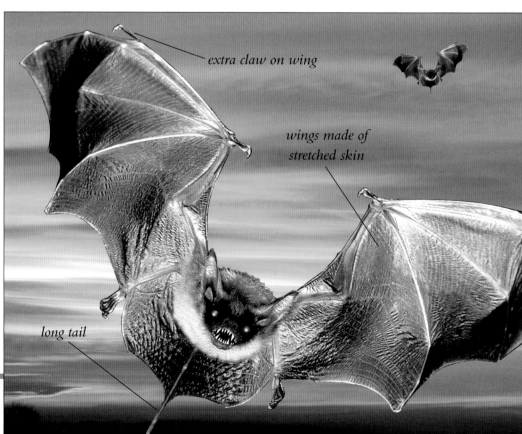

extra claw on wing

wings made of stretched skin

long tail

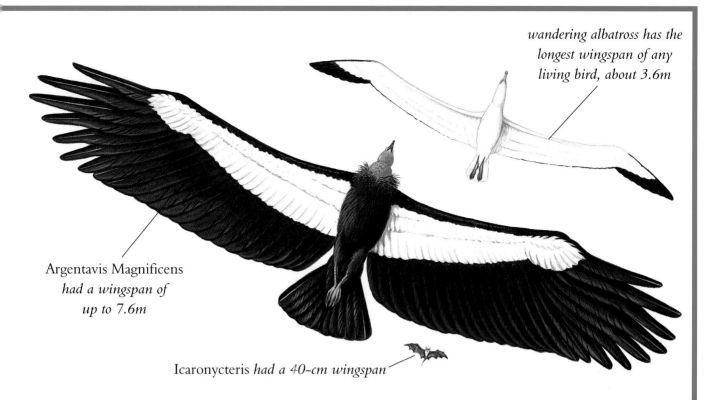

wandering albatross has the longest wingspan of any living bird, about 3.6m

Argentavis Magnificens had a wingspan of up to 7.6m

Icaronycteris *had a 40-cm wingspan*

Since the *Archaeopteryx*, birds have developed into a very successful animal group. Today there are nearly 9000 kinds, but none is as big as the huge *Argentavis Magnificens* that once soared over the grassy plains of South America.

▲ *Argentavis* lived about 6 million years ago. It was bigger than any flying bird today.

DINOSAURS IN DISGUISE

How did birds survive after the pterosaurs and dinosaurs died out? The answer is that we don't know. It is still a mystery why some forms of life survived the great disaster of 65 million years ago, while many others were killed off completely.

But, as most experts now agree that early birds had dinosaur ancestors, it seems that the dinosaurs are still with us!

FLYING WORDS

Here are some technical terms used in this book.

crest

▲ The *Phobetor*'s head crest was long and bony.

carcass
The body of a dead animal.

cold-blooded
An animal, such as a reptile or a fish, with blood that matches the temperature of its surroundings. To get active after a cold night, a reptile has to warm up in the Sun. A warm-blooded animal, such as a bat or human, has blood that stays at the same temperature constantly, so it does not slow down in the cold.

crest
Outgrowth on a pterosaur's or bird's head. Bony pterosaur crests helped balance in flight. Feathered bird crests are often used in courtship displays.

dinobird
Remains found in China that show a mixture of dinosaur and bird features.

dinosaur
Land-dwelling reptiles that lived between 225 and 65 million years ago. Most experts think they died out after a huge meteor strike.

fossil
The remains of a living thing preserved in rock.

membrane
A thin, flexible layer of living tissue. The thin, lightweight wings of pterosaurs were made of membranes, and so are bats' wings today.

mammal
A warm-blooded animal that has hair or fur and that feeds its young with milk produced in the mother's body. Bats are flying mammals.

meteor
A chunk of rock hurtling through space, ranging in size from tiny grains to flying mountains many kilometres across. One of these, colliding with the Earth, is thought to have killed off the pterosaurs and dinosaurs.

prey
An animal that is hunted by another animal for food.

puffin
Sea bird with a coloured beak, thought to look like that of the *Eudimorphodon* pterosoar.

reptile
An animal such as a crocodile that is covered with scales or horny plates. Reptiles are usually cold-blooded and lay

shelled eggs on land, rather than giving birth to live young. Pterosaurs and dinosaurs were prehistoric reptiles, but scientists think pterosaurs had fur not scales.

wingspan

The tip-to-tip width of a flying creature's wings when they are fully stretched out.

WEIRD WORDS

This pronunciation guide should help you say the names of flying creatures.

Anhanguerra
an-hang-wear-er

Anurognathus
an-er-onya-thus

Archaeopteryx
ark-ee-opt-ter-iks

Argentavis magnificens
arj-ent-arv-is mag-nif-iss-ens

Baptornis
bap-torn-is

Coelurosauravus
see-lure-oh-sore-ay-vus

Ctenochasma
ten-oh-kaz-ma

Dimorphodon
die-morf-oh-don

Draco volans
dray-ko vo-lanz

Dsungariterus
sun-gar-it-air-us

Eudimorphodon
you-dee-morf-oh-don

Gastornis
gas-torn-is

Gnathosaurus
nat-oh-sore-us

Icaronycteris
eye-car-on-ikt-er-is

Longisquama
lon-iss-kwar-ma

Meganeura
mega-ner-ah

Ornithocheirus
orn-ee-tho-kear-us

Peteinosaurus
pet-eye-no-sore-us

Phobetor
foe-beet-or

Phorusrhacos
four-us-rak-os

Propalaeotherium
pro-pal-ee-oh-theer-ee-um

Pteranodon ingens
ter-an-oh-don in-jens

Pteranodon sternbergi
ter-an-oh-don stern-berg-ee

Pterodactyl elegans
ter-oh-dak-til ell-ee-ganz

Pterodaustro
ter-oh-door-stroh

Quetzalcoatlus
kwet-sal-coat-lus

Rhamphorynchus
ram-four-ink-us

Sordes pilosus
sword-es pill-oh-sus

Tropeognathus
tro-pee-on-ath-us

▲ A dinobird with four feathered wings was discovered in 2003.

FLYING FACTS

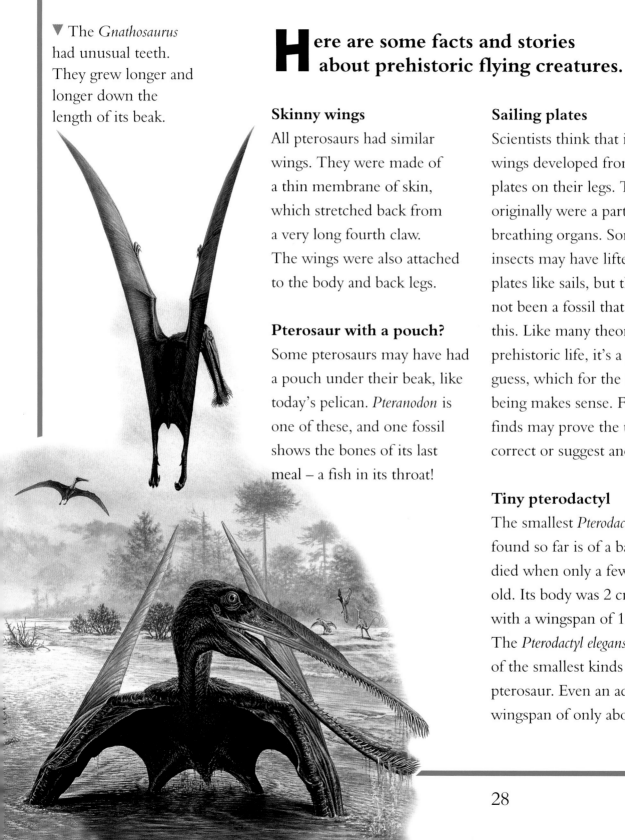

▼ The *Gnathosaurus* had unusual teeth. They grew longer and longer down the length of its beak.

Here are some facts and stories about prehistoric flying creatures.

Skinny wings

All pterosaurs had similar wings. They were made of a thin membrane of skin, which stretched back from a very long fourth claw. The wings were also attached to the body and back legs.

Pterosaur with a pouch?

Some pterosaurs may have had a pouch under their beak, like today's pelican. *Pteranodon* is one of these, and one fossil shows the bones of its last meal – a fish in its throat!

Sailing plates

Scientists think that insect wings developed from large plates on their legs. These originally were a part of the breathing organs. Some early insects may have lifted their plates like sails, but there has not been a fossil that shows this. Like many theories about prehistoric life, it's a good guess, which for the time being makes sense. Future finds may prove the theory is correct or suggest another idea.

Tiny pterodactyl

The smallest *Pterodactyl* fossil found so far is of a baby that died when only a few weeks old. Its body was 2 cm long, with a wingspan of 18 cm. The *Pterodactyl elegans* was one of the smallest kinds of pterosaur. Even an adult had a wingspan of only about 25 cm.

World travellers

There were long-distance air travellers a long time before the tourists of today. Starting more than 200 million years ago, pterosaurs flew the world. Their remains have been found almost everywhere.

◀ Only one fossil has ever been found of this little pterosaur, the *Anurognathus*. It had a skull just 3 cm long and is shown here trying to catch a prehistoric wasp.

Most flyers

There are more flying insects on Earth than any other kind of animal. Some (such as the cockroach) have changed very little for 300 million years.

Fish grabber

Rhamphorynchus (see page 2) probably lived along seashores, like today's seagulls. It had forward-pointing teeth so it could 'stab and grab' fish, gulping them down headfirst.

Free lunch

A series of lagoons in northeast Brazil once teemed with fish. Scientists have found remains of more than 20 kinds of pterosaur that flew in from far and wide to feast on the fish!

Batty facts

Early bats soon split into two groups – small microbats and larger megabats. Bats today range from the tiny pipistrelle, with a wingspan of just 7 cm, to the larger 1.2m-wingspan flying fox. Bats are mammals, but they share one thing with the reptilian pterosaurs – their wings are also made of a thin membrane of skin.

Legging along

Unless you could fly, it was dangerous to stray near one of the huge flightless birds of South America 40 million years ago. *Gastornis* could run after prey at about 60 km/h!

FLYING CREATURES SUMMARY

The first creatures to develop flapping-wing flight were insects that lived about 300 million years ago.

The biggest flying insect was *Meganeura*, a dragonfly with wings 70 cm across. Reptiles took to the air 250 million years ago, but the earliest ones could only glide rather than take off from the ground. Early pterosaurs flew about 220 million years ago. The biggest pterosaur was *Quetzalcoatlus*, which had a wingspan of up to 12m. *Archaeopteryx* was the first bird, but some later birds did not fly at all. *Gastornis* was a fierce, flightless bird that lived about 40 million years ago and was 2m tall. The biggest flying bird was the South American *Argentavis* of about 6 million years ago. Bats were the most recent kind of animal to develop flapping-wing flight, but they are mammals, not birds.

▼ Museums often have life-size models of prehistoric animals, here an *Archaeopteryx* just landing. These models give you a good idea of how the animals might have looked in real life.

FLYING CREATURES ON THE WEB

You can find information on prehistoric flying creatures on the Internet. Use a search engine for a general hunt around, or type in the name of a particular animal you want to find out about. Here are some good sites to start with:

▼ There are some good sites that have information on flying creatures. Here are three screenshots.

http://www.dinodata.net
A good starting point for finding out about dinosaurs, and the site also has some good information on pterosaurs.

http://www.pterosaur.org
Lots of information on this site, including full details of a company that makes life-sized flying model pterosaurs! You can see a sample of one of these amazing models in the picture at right.

http://sciam.com
The home site of the respected magazine *Scientific American*. Has a good search engine that you can use to track down information.

http://www.bbc.co.uk/beasts
This is a small part of the BBC's massive site, here providing a wealth of material related to the TV series, *Walking with Beasts*. A related BBC website also has pages devoted to pterosaurs. Find it on the **http://www.bbc.co.uk/dinosaurs**

INDEX